So Tell Me

So Tell Me

A Primer for Vocational Ministry Applicants

JONATHAN FEATHERS

RESOURCE *Publications* • Eugene, Oregon

SO TELL ME
A Primer for Vocational Ministry Applicants

Copyright © 2016 Jonathan Feathers. All rights reserved. Except for brief quotations in critical publications or reviews, no part of this book may be reproduced in any manner without prior written permission from the publisher. Write: Permissions, Wipf and Stock Publishers, 199 W. 8th Ave., Suite 3, Eugene, OR 97401.

Resource Publications
An Imprint of Wipf and Stock Publishers
199 W. 8th Ave., Suite 3
Eugene, OR 97401

www.wipfandstock.com

PAPERBACK ISBN: 978-1-4982-8444-8
HARDCOVER ISBN: 978-1-4982-8446-2
EBOOK ISBN: 978-1-4982-8445-5

Manufactured in the U.S.A.   11/04/16

For the churches who have helped me
discover my ministry.

Contents

Introduction: So Tell Me | ix

Chapter One
What is the vision of the church? | 1

Chapter Two
What is the mission of the church? | 4

Chapter Three
What are the goals of the church? | 7

Chapter Four
What are the ministry teams? | 10

Chapter Five
What is the expected level of (member) involvement? | 13

Chapter Six
What is the mission's (locally and/or globally) budget? | 16

Chapter Seven
What are the three most important qualities of the church? | 19

Chapter Eight
What does the church do well? | 22

Chapter Nine
What is the church known for in the community? | 25

Chapter Ten
How would you describe the health of the church? | 28

Chapter Eleven
How would you describe the demographic of the church? | 31

Chapter Twelve
What is the line of authority? | 34

Chapter Thirteen
Is there a ministry budget to work from? | 37

Chapter Fourteen
Is there a statement of faith? | 40

Chapter Fifteen
Are there any major conflicts? | 43

Chapter Sixteen
What is the job description? | 46

Chapter Seventeen
What is the organizational chart? | 49

Chapter Eighteen
What is the role of elders and/or deacons? | 52

Chapter Nineteen
What is the relationship between elders and/or deacons with the minister? | 55

Chapter Twenty
Is the minister expected to attend everything? | 58

Chapter Twenty One
Why did the last minister leave? | 61

Chapter Twenty Two
Are there leadership development standards? | 64

Chapter Twenty Three
How are polices developed? | 67

Chapter Twenty Four
How are policies implemented? | 70

Appendix: Checklist | 73

Introduction

So Tell Me

Job hunting can be a daunting task for both the interviewing personnel team and the applicant. The search process for vocational ministers can span the length of months, potentially even years, depending upon the position. Like most job hunting processes, there is a job posting, followed by several interviews, until the job is extended to the applicant. The interviewer is asking questions and determining if the applicant is a good fit within their organization or church. For churches, the process is lengthened due to the many facets of vocational ministry and the composition of the church.

One of the most common interviewing questions revolves around the phrase, "so tell me." The interviewer gains remarkable insight about the applicant and the position for which he or she is applying through this phase, "so tell me." As an applicant, have you ever stopped to consider that question or phrase as though you were asking the interviewer? This book is about asking the interviewer, especially churches, a number of questions to determine if the

So Tell Me

church is a right fit for you. Throughout this book, a series of questions are posed for the applicant to ask or research to help determine if the church is the right fit for the position to which the applicant is applying. This book is a primer for vocational ministry applicants to consider for him or herself these questions on some level; some questions may bear more weight than any others. This book might encourage or generate the applicant's ability to develop a number of questions on his or her own. The answers received or the research uncovered through these questions will help the applicant determine if the church is a good fit for his or her interests, passions, and skills. Each chapter poses a question, explains what the question is about, and I discuss why the question is important. This provides a practical perspective to the question. It is my hope that this book will assist you in discovering the position and church in which you can serve Christ.

Chapter One

What is the vision of the church?

What is the vision of the church? This question seeks to clarify the vision and long-term objectives and goals of the church. What does the church hope to accomplish in the future? This is not clear for many churches. For those with a vision, it can be energizing. Many churches possess a vision, or at least did, when the church was established. The church began with a vision in hope of achieving or accomplishing something that could take years to complete.

For the church, an applicant is identifying whether there is a formal vision that has been recorded and communicated. Either the church has a clear vision that has been recorded and communicated consistently, or it does not. Vision seeks to explain the direction of what the church is striving to achieve, attain, or complete. The vision may be abstract, serving as a distant star, or concrete, relating to something measurable. With this question, the applicant can determine whether he/she agrees with the vision of the church. If a vision is not stated, then this may affect the applicant's decision. He or she may see this as an opportunity to cast a vision or look elsewhere.

I ask this question to determine if the previous or current leadership has considered a vision for the church. If a vision is stated, does the vision align and resonate with me? Is the vision one in which I want to fully support and get behind? If a vision is not stated, do I believe and feel this is the right time and place to develop a vision for this church or organization? Will this position give me a chance to engage in fulfilling the vision?

Whether an applicant is considering a church or organization, a clear vision becomes a starting point to determine whether this church or organization is a good fit.

Questions for reflection:
(Record your responses below.)

So tell me, what is the vision of this church?

Why would I ask about vision?

Have I researched an answer to this question?
(For instance, is an answer to this question posted on a website or publication?)

Chapter Two

What is the mission of the church?

What is the mission of the church? This is a basic question regarding the reason for existence. Why does a church exist? This seems to be a simple question, but it must be answered. Each church will and should be able to articulate this in at least one sentence. The answer to this question explains why a particular church exists.

For the church, an applicant is determining whether a particular church has defined its mission and if it has been communicated consistently. Unfortunately, some churches do not have this defined. Even if a church does, then the mission is not always communicated consistently among staff and congregants. At an applicant interview for a position within an existing church, he or she should consider this question and its answer to determine if it resonates within him or her. An applicant should consider if the position in the particular church is even worth applying for. If the mission is not stated or communicated, it may be a

What is the mission of the church?

unique opportunity for the church to visit, clarify, and begin communicating.

I ask this question to see if the church or organization has determined and/or communicates the mission. The answer to this question allows me to see whether I agree with it. As stated in chapter one, do I believe and feel this is the right time and place to develop a mission for this church or organization? Will the position which I am applying for allow me a chance to collaborate and clarify the mission?

Whether an applicant is considering a church or organization, a well defined mission helps the applicant decide if it is a good fit.

Questions for reflection:
(Record your responses below.)

So tell me, what is the defined mission?

Why would I ask about the mission?

Have I researched an answer to this question?
(For instance, is an answer to this question posted on a website or publication?)

Chapter Three

What are the goals of the church?

What are the goals of the church? Bear in mind that if this is a church plant or young church, an applicant would be heavily involved in developing the long and short range goals. However, if this is an existing church, the applicant should be inquiring about the work that is to be done and what goals are to be achieved. Although some experts may differ on the use of the terminology of goals and objectives, there is a consensus that, at some point, goals and/or objectives need to be concrete rather than abstract, clearly defined and evaluated. Other factors to be included are measurable components and the timeframe within which goals and objectives are to be achieved.

For the applicant: does the church state its short and long range goals? What is the theme for the year, or other designated time period? What activities, programs, resources and tools are needed to achieve the short range goals? What is needed for the long range goals? The applicant should also be sensitive as to whether goals and objectives are already stated for the particular position being applied for, or if the goals and objectives would be defined once beginning the position. As the applicant becomes aware of the goals and objectives, he or she can begin to understand his or her expectations and how the work will connect to the larger scope and vision of the organization.

I ask this question to see if the church is focusing on a specific goal and objective both short-term and long-term. It helps me decipher where the current leadership stands and what steps need to be addressed. If you aim at nothing, you will hit nothing. When it comes to churches, there is a sensitivity to where God's Spirit may be leading. However, I believe it is appropriate to set goals and objectives that are in tune with God.

Questions for reflection:
(Record your responses below.)

So tell me, what are the goals and objectives?

Why would I ask about goals and objectives?

Have I researched an answer to this question?
(For instance, is an answer to this question posted on a website or publication?)

Chapter Four

What are the ministry teams?

What are the ministry teams? This question asks about the volunteer opportunities that are established. If ministry teams are established, then what are the expectations for the team and its participants? If ministry teams are not established, then what teams need to be developed? More teams provide more opportunities for people to get involved and connected with the mission of the church. The purpose and function of the teams provide people with the opportunity to discover how they can contribute to the mission of the church and engage in the life of the church.

An applicant should consider what roles exist for people to volunteer in and what is expected. It would also prove helpful to know the statistics of volunteer opportunities and how many people are serving in the opportunities. By knowing these facts, an assessment can be made to determine what new roles and new teams need to be identified and how many people are actively engaged in those roles or needed for new opportunities. By being aware of this, an applicant can determine what needs to be done.

What are the ministry teams?

I ask this question to determine if people in the church are actively engaged in the life of the church. If not, why not? If so, wonderful. This helps me identify what needs to be communicated and what types of ministry team's recruitment need to take place. Granted, there are outside factors which may affect this as well, but this is one step closer in knowing if this church is the right fit for me along with how I can best serve and lead in this church. Every church is different, but by getting a baseline assessment on where things are, then one can lead to where it needs to be in the area of ministry teams. More participants lead to more teams and more opportunities to get involved.

Questions for reflection:
(Record your responses below.)

So tell me, what are the ministry teams?

Why would I ask about ministry teams?

Have I researched an answer to this question?
(For instance, is an answer to this question posted on a website or publication?)

Chapter Five

What is the expected level of (member) involvement?

What is the expected level of (member) involvement? This may seem like an odd question, but it must be asked. This is an important question because it gets to the heart of the matter, which is—what is expected of me as a member of your church? Many times people do not know what is expected. Once the expectation is clarified, then people begin to get a sense of direction of where they need to go and how to get there. Many churches do not communicate what is expected of their members. This is why so many wonder why people are not involved. Sometimes, it just takes communicating an expectation and description of opportunities that people can rise to. Once the expectation, or expectations, are identified and communicated, then people understand what is expected of them. Then the next logical course of action is helping and equipping people to take the next step so they can meet the expectation.

An applicant should consider this question because it helps in identifying where people are in their involvement within the church. As noted earlier, each of these questions is a tool in helping the applicant determine if the church is a right fit for him or her. Many of these questions can help the applicant determine where people are in order to lead people to where they need to be. A clear set of identifiable expectations can help members and even nonmembers understand what they need to do in response to their involvement within the church. The involvement often ties into the discipleship process of a respective church.

I ask this question to better understand how involved the members of the church are. Sometimes, there are too many unrealistic expectations, but most often expectations are not identified or clearly communicated.

Questions for reflection:
(Record your responses below.)

So tell me, are member expectations defined?

Why would I ask about member expectations?

Have I researched an answer to this question?
(For instance, is an answer to this question posted on a website or publication?)

Chapter Six

What is the mission's (locally and/or globally) budget?

What is the mission's (locally and/or globally) budget? This question uncovers several things. One, does the church invest in the local community? Two, does the church invest in the global community? These two questions may be answered by an actual dollar amount or percentage. These questions may also be answered by who or what organization is supported by said dollars. Some churches do not factor in a dollar amount, or percentage, of reaching their communities and then the churches wonder why they struggle. It is because there is not a community presence. On the other hand, some churches give ten to twenty-five percent of their annual operating budget to support the local and/or global community.

An applicant should ask this question because he or she can determine how much the church invests or supports the local and or global community. For some applicants, this will challenge them to find ways to build on the

What is the mission's (locally and/or globally) budget?

level of engagement and awareness; for others it will usher in a way to raise the bar and others will look elsewhere. This may even give the applicant an opportunity to network with others and respond to needs and crises that may arise.

I ask this question because it tells me how much the church thinks of others in various contexts. I realize there are often economic challenges and struggles when it comes to giving units, but does the church engage the community at any level? I have heard of churches spending upwards to 75 percent of their annual budget on personnel while leaving the remaining 25 percent to tackle operating expenses and local and/or global missions. A mission's budget reminds me of the partnership with the global mission of the church and ways in which we partner with others on so many levels.

Questions for reflection:
(Record your responses below.)

So tell me, what is the mission's budget?

Why would I ask about a mission's budget?

Have I researched an answer to this question?
(For instance, is an answer to this question posted on a website or publication?)

Chapter Seven

What are the three most important qualities of the church?

What are the three most important qualities of the church? This question inquires about the perception of the church both internally and externally. This is worth investigating because it makes one ponder whether any research has been done to determine what this particular church is known for and does well. It is vital for the church to identify its strengths, as seen inside and outside the church, and capitalize on those strengths. For instance, if the church says outreach is a strong quality, then how is it demonstrated? Is this statement backed up with strong evidences or practices?

The applicant should consider asking and researching this question regarding the church. By doing so, the applicant will be better informed of this particular church. If this question is unclear or seems to be unresolved, then this may provide an opportunity for the applicant to uncover these qualities as well as develop the qualities. It really does come down to a matter of preference or opinion. Some would prefer that these qualities already be evidenced, while others see this would be a great way to discover and develop new qualities.

I ask this question to see if these qualities mesh with my interests and passions. If the qualities do not align with me, then that tells me something. If the qualities align with me, then that tells me something. If some of the qualities align and others do not align with me, then that tells me something as well. This becomes another factor in the decision process. I must decide whether to be at peace with the information, seek compromise, or determine how much weight this information will carry with the overall decision of "do I want to become a part of the ministry team or not." By assessing the qualities of the church from what insiders and outsiders would say, the applicant has a deeper understanding of what has been done and what should be done.

Questions for reflection:
(Record your responses below.)

So tell me, do the qualities resonate with me?

Why would I ask about qualities of the church?

Have I researched an answer to this question?
(For instance, is an answer to this question posted on a website or publication?)

Chapter Eight

What does the church do well?

What does the church do well? This question ties very closely with the previous question—what are the three most important qualities of the church? Qualities would be defined as abstract. For instance, the church is friendly. This would be an abstract quality, whereas this question addresses concrete actions. For instance, this church does children's ministry well. This can be determined by the energy level, excitement, creativity, ways in which children are ministered to, and the amount of budget dedicated to this area. This can appear in numerous ways: children, students, adults, education, music, and community involvement, just to name a few.

The applicant is deciding whether this church has been doing something well, and, if so, what is it? If not, why not? Perhaps, the applicant is looking for a challenge to do something well, discover it, build it, and develop it. The more questions an applicant asks or considers will help him or her to determine if this church is a good fit. The applicant must keep in mind that the interviewing church will

What does the church do well?

be asking questions as well to see if the applicant is a good fit for this church.

I ask this question to determine the self awareness of the church. Perhaps what is done well is based on previous years and former leadership. Perhaps what is done is not really clear. This helps me see if there are realistic or unrealistic expectations that have been set or projected upon the applicant. I ask myself whether I can fully support what has been done well, or is the leadership open to refinement? Unfortunately, budgets reflect where resources are going and, at times, resources need to be redirected. When this happens, results are often what people did not expect. Resources may not be allocated where they need to be.

Questions for reflection:
(Record your responses below.)

So tell me, what is done well?

Why would I ask about what is done well?

Have I researched an answer to this question?
(For instance, is an answer to this question posted on a website or publication?)

Chapter Nine

What is the church known for in the community?

What is the church known for in the community? This question scratches the surface as to how outsiders perceive the church to which one is applying. What is the response of others? How do they view this church? Have they even heard of this church? By asking these questions, one can begin to discern the involvement of the church within the community. It begs one to consider how is the community view of the church measured? Any responses may purely be observational, but it does give some insight on the interaction with people who may not be active participants or members.

An applicant begins to get a sense of whether this church is in tune with its community. By asking this question, an applicant can gauge how active the church is in reaching its non-members. Buzzwords give an insight on the health of the church. Positive words such as friendly, hospitable, and engaging, evoke one perspective. Negative words such as boring, cold, and dead evoke another perspective. Such words can be helpful for the applicant to discover his or her place with this church and what he or she can bring to this church.

I ask this question to determine if the church is open to receiving feedback. I like to know if the church evaluates its philosophy, its ministries, and its community involvement, just to name a few. Feedback positively and critically can help with assessing what needs to be corrected or improved. By comparing what members and non-attendees say can help determine if they are truly aware of the people the church is trying to reach. For the applicant, it continues deciphering if the church is the right fit. All of these questions may not be answered. Therefore, this may very well be the kind of challenge and calling the applicant is looking for. The applicant may be an instrument to change from being described as cold to exciting.

Questions for reflection:
(Record your responses below.)

So tell me, what is the church known for in the community?

Why would I ask about what the church is known for in the community?

Have I researched an answer to this question?
(For instance, is an answer to this question posted on a website or publication?)

Chapter Ten

How would you describe the health of the church?

How would you describe the health of the church? Quality is an important measurement. The previous question looks at quality from an outside perspective, while this question looks at quality from an internal perspective. Consider a visit to the doctor's office. The doctor can make a diagnosis based solely on observation. However, when additional testing is used, such as blood work, then a more accurate diagnosis can be identified. For instance, swelling may be noticed on the outside, but after testing, it is determined that the swelling is due to an infection on the inside.

An applicant may ask questions regarding a description of the health of the church. Sometimes leadership will fully disclose, while others reveal a little at a time. The applicant may be looking for quantitative measurements, such as what is the number of adults who attend the worship services, how many of those adults are involved in a group or class, and how many of those volunteer with a ministry

How would you describe the health of the church?

team? Looking at quantitative measurements leads to qualitative. This can encourage deeper analysis of why people are connecting or not connecting. Other factors may exist which affect the health of the church such as personalities and unity.

I ask this question to learn more about the church that I am not already familiar with. On one interview, the search team described that a small percentage does a majority of the work and that they multi-task. This indicates a recipe for burnout. By asking this question, I was able to better grasp their situation and what this church was looking for. I consider two aspects: how can ministry improve and grow and what is keeping ministry from improving and growing. As a doctor runs test to diagnose and treat the patient, I inquire about the health status from the patient (church) to diagnose and treat.

Questions for reflection:
(Record your responses below.)

So tell me, what is the health of the church?

Why would I ask about the health of the church?

Have I researched an answer to this question?
(For instance, is an answer to this question posted on a website or publication?)

Chapter Eleven

How would you describe the demographic of the church?

How would you describe the demographic of the church? This question serves as an analysis of the status of the current demographic of the church of which the applicant applies. There is no right or wrong answer, but the information serves as a tool in understanding the composition of the people of the church. The information becomes useful when making ministry plans and casting vision. For instance, if the demographic is of a certain age, then ministries could be designed to address those ages or the lack thereof. If the demographic reflects that a large employer in the community has closed, then ministries may address the psychological and emotional side of this impact.

It is important for the applicant to gather as much information regarding the demographic trends of the church in order to prepare for ways to minister to the demographic trends of the community. Every church is unique. Every culture is unique. The applicant should be considering the uniqueness of the culture of the church, the culture of the leadership, and the culture of the community in which the church exists. The culture ties in with the demographics. Demographics include a number of strata such as: population, education, cost of living, healthcare, employers, and community heritage, just to name some.

I ask this question to see if the interviewing team is aware of what has and is taking place within the church as well as the community. Do the responses mesh with the research? For instance, a response may be "this is a good place to live," but a majority of the residents are retiring. This may be true on one hand, but on the other hand, does it hold up under the number of schools and adolescents that reside in the community? It is a good place to live from one perspective, but from another perspective a young family would be wondering about local schools. An applicant should be informing himself or herself along with discerning if this is the right fit for ministry.

Questions for reflection:
(Record your responses below.)

So tell me, what are the demographic trends of the church and community?

Why would I ask about demographics?

Have I researched an answer to this question?
(For instance, is an answer to this question posted on a website or publication?)

Chapter Twelve

What is the line of authority?

What is the line of authority? This question digs within the organizational infrastructure. Is there a clear path or line of authority? This needs to be made clear. Churches need to clarify and document this. For instance, some churches allow greater authority to the lay leadership over the paid staff. For instance, I served in a church where I had a budget; however, I could hardly spend any money. If one hundred dollars was to be spent, then it had to be approved by the board. This process stifled ministry. In another example, the staff was led to believe that each staff reported to the lay leadership. In other words, every paid staff reported to lay leadership. A clear line of authority must be developed.

An applicant needs to be sure of the line of authority. Who does the open position report to? Who is responsible for direct reports? If possible, try and decipher how often the organizational infrastructure changes. For some, this is reviewed at incremental growth stages. For others, the organizational infrastructure changes yearly. This creates

What is the line of authority?

tension and confusion. Some applicants desire more responsibility while others do not.

I ask this question to assess maturity levels. I served in one church where it was verbally indicated that I would oversee paid staff and day to day operations. I then came to find out that the lay leadership conducted reviews without my input and did not honor the line of authority that was agreed upon and communicated. This added frustration and tension to all. I prefer a clear line of authority to be fully understood to alleviate any confusion. If the organizational infrastructure constantly changes, then how is it able to withstand the test of time?

Questions for reflection:
(Record your responses below.)

So tell me, what is the line of authority?

Why would I ask about the line of authority?

Have I researched an answer to this question?
(For instance, is an answer to this question posted on a website or publication?)

Chapter Thirteen

Is there a ministry budget to work from?

Is there a ministry budget to work from? This may seem like an odd question to ask to begin with, but it should be done. For the position to which the applicant is applying for, are there resources, specifically financial resources, available for the person to fulfill the job? Some churches budget for certain areas such as a children's budget, or line item, that is to be used for children's ministry in order to purchase curriculum, advertise, and program needs. I have served in capacities where a budget was not available to conduct ministry. This made it exceptionally difficult when it was needed to purchase curriculum or food for an event.

An applicant should inquire about the ministry budget for the position along with the overall budget. If financial resources are available, then how much? Who decides on how to spend the budget? What is the process for approval of the budget? How does one make purchases? Is a credit card used? Is there a reimbursement policy? How soon do checks need to be requested to make a payment to vendors? These may seem like detail oriented questions, but it can affect the efficiency and effectiveness of ministry. If limited funds are available, then the applicant has to get creative about financial resources. Financial resources may very well determine the priority of certain ministry needs and events. Living in a digital world with a plethora of resources available, one still has to factor in certain expenses.

I ask this question because I have experienced how difficult it can be to conduct ministry out of my own pocket along with everyday living expenses. A budget alleviates any personal expenses for ministry. There should be a defined practice of how money is transacted and held accountable. For instance, are there receipts to document expenses? An applicant should take note of the resources that are available because expenses can add up fast. When there is a downturn in income, this affects the budget as well and all parties should be prepared to make the necessary adjustments. I have served on a staff where all accounts were placed on hold. Many of these details will probably be addressed when needed.

Questions for reflection:
(Record your responses below.)

So tell me, what is the ministry budget?

Why would I ask about a ministry budget?

Have I researched an answer to this question?
(For instance, is an answer to this question posted on a website or publication?)

Chapter Fourteen

Is there a statement of faith?

Is there a statement of faith? This may seem like an obvious question, but it should be considered. Some people will apply for an open position without identifying, knowing, or understanding what the church believes and or why. Therefore, an applicant could find himself or herself in a situation where ministry practices are conducted that go against his or her beliefs. Would you be willing to join or participate in something that you did not believe in or fully support? When it comes to churches, there are often varying beliefs and practices in denominational and non-denominational churches. It is important that the applicant educate himself or herself on these.

Most of the time during the interviewing stages, a church will inquire about an applicant's statement of belief on predetermined areas. I believe the applicant should be researching and asking as well. An applicant may be concerned about the statement of beliefs. Throughout life, an applicant may hold to certain beliefs strongly while others have changed their viewpoints. An applicant needs to be

Is there a statement of faith?

aware of what he or she believes and if those stated beliefs align with the church and the position.

I ask this question to determine if the beliefs of the church to which I have applied, and my beliefs align. A majority of the time, there is alignment and agreement. There have been instances where a belief was different. This became a factor in my decision making process. If I discovered differing beliefs, then could I continue with the interviewing process and fully support the beliefs? By asking questions, I hope to make a well informed decision within in the whole search process.

Questions for reflection:
(Record your responses below.)

So tell me, what is the statement of faith?

Why would I ask about the statement of faith?

Have I researched an answer to this question?
(For instance, is an answer to this question posted on a website or publication?)

Chapter Fifteen

Are there any major conflicts?

Are there any major conflicts in the past or currently? To some, this may seem like a bold question to ask. I think about it in terms of honesty and transparency. Does it seem as though the church responds honestly? Is anything disguised? Does the question seem to be avoided? It is helpful to know what an applicant may be facing. If there was a major conflict, how did this occur? How recent is it? All of these weigh in on how ministry will be conducted. If there was a recent incident, then how will the church respond to a new staff coming aboard? A lot of stresses, pressures, and unrealistic expectations may be projected on new staff. I was once on staff that had a conflict in the past. Upon my arrival, this incident occurred about 15 years prior. However, the effects of the incident still lingered and had not been dealt with. I found myself ministering to this church. In order to move forward, this incident had to be addressed.

An applicant may tread cautiously when contemplating this question. In order to become familiar, one needs to ask questions. Some of these questions may come up naturally in other conversations or informal interviews. The applicant should be attuned and aware of what questions exist and what information needs to be discovered. Any caution flags that may pop up can help the applicant decide if the church is a good fit. It may very well mean the applicant is called to this place to build and repair.

As I have asked, this question informs me as to how transparent those I am interviewing with are. The search team has a great task to find a candidate. Is the search team representing the church well? Trust takes time. If details are hidden from the onset, then it may take longer to build honesty, transparency and trust.

Questions for reflection:
(Record your responses below.)

So tell me, has a major conflict occurred in the past or recently?

Why would I ask about conflict?

Have I researched an answer to this question?
(For instance, is an answer to this question posted on a website or publication?)

Chapter Sixteen

What is the job description?

What is the job description? One would think that this is an obvious question. If there is a job posting regarding an open position, then the job description must already be clear. Not always. I have served churches that posted the job opening with its title, but found out later that the position included a number of other items which became a standard of unrealistic expectations. It seemed forty hours were expected in the office plus other activities. Ministry lends itself to seasons of long work hours, but a balance is needed to maintain physical, emotional, spiritual, and even relational health.

An applicant should inquire about a specific documented job description. By doing so, the applicant becomes more familiar with the position and the work that has been done. Upon reviewing the job description, the applicant becomes more aware of the details of the job and what is expected within the church. If the applicant is hired and possesses additional knowledge, skills and abilities, then

What is the job description?

the job description may eventually be edited for the person in the position.

I ask this question to obtain a copy of the current working job description. It gives me additional insight into the position that I am applying for. I have served on a staff without a formal job description. By not having a job description, there were not clear expectations set for anyone, nor was there a method of accountability. I have also served on a staff where the job description did not include many other items expected of the person filling the position, which made the position unrealistic. By having a clear job description in the beginning, many potential concerns could be avoided. A job description creates an understanding between the employer and employee. Be prepared to discuss any phrase that begins with, "and any other duties assigned."

Questions for reflection:
(Record your responses below.)

So tell me, what is the job description?

Why would I ask about a job description?

Have I researched an answer to this question?
(For instance, is an answer to this question posted on a website or publication?)

Chapter Seventeen

What is the organizational chart?

What is the organizational chart? An organizational chart illustrates the reporting structure of the personnel. This can vary greatly from church to church or from organization to organization. It is important for a church to illustrate these lines of authority because it may get confusing or even cross depending upon the work that is to be done. An organizational chart for a church of less than 300 may look differently than one of a church of over two thousand. It could prove beneficial for an organizational chart to even exist for volunteers.

An applicant should consider the organizational chart of the church. It informs the candidate of who he or she will be reporting to along with an understanding of any direct reports reporting to the applicant. By documenting an organizational chart, one can also see how team members function within the respective roles. It would also be worth noting to ask when the last time the organizational chart was last updated or modified. On the same line, inquire about how frequently the organizational chart changes. Ministry leaders make adjustments as needed and even frequently at times. If the organizational chart changes often, then the leadership may be in question, communication breaks down, and tension can build as well as position descriptions losing accuracy and relevance. The system becomes at risk and dysfunctional.

I ask the question to see if this has been thought of or even developed. The more insight I receive of what takes place within the organizational chart, the better I am prepared to lead. A consistently changing organization chart can leave any staff and volunteers feeling a little apprehensive. An informed leader scouts. Any details of the previous staffing structure may affect the future staffing structure. I believe a strong organizational chart does not change constantly. Picture a home with walls. If the walls keep moving the roof could collapse.

Questions for reflection:
(Record your responses below.)

So tell me, where will I fit on the organizational chart?

Why would I ask about the organizational chart?

Have I researched an answer to this question?
(For instance, is an answer to this question posted on a website or publication?)

Chapter Eighteen

What is the role of elders and/or deacons?

What is the role of elders and/or deacons? In many churches, the role of elders and/or deacons refers to the lay leadership. Depending upon the history of the church, the by-laws, or denomination, these roles are used or something similar. In some churches, it is the volunteer base. How do the roles of elders and deacons interact with the paid church staff? This question ties in with the organizational chart. Where does the line of authority lie and how is it communicated?

An applicant needs to be informed of the roles of elders and/or deacons and the working relationship with the paid church staff position. Many of the people who serve in these capacities do so, on a volunteer level. Perhaps, recruitment and training have been conducted for these roles. Sometimes equipping does not take place. Volunteers, elders, deacons, and paid staff often float around without any accountability or structure. As the applicant considers

What is the role of elders and/or deacons?

whether the church is a potential good fit, the applicant may consider asking about such roles and relationships, especially in an established church. For a young church or even a church plant, the roles and relationships will look very differently. Nonetheless, it would help an applicant be aware of what exists or could be developed.

I ask this question to understand the roles, relationships and reporting structure of a church. On one hand, I have experienced a church where these roles were not very clearly-defined or organized. On the other hand, I have experienced a church where these roles were very clearly-defined and a strong relationship existed. I have seen the tensions, checks and balances. For a senior leader position, the applicant should be looking at all facets because it can determine the readiness for change.

Questions for reflection:
(Record your responses below.)

So tell me, what is the role of elders and/or deacons?

Why would I ask about elders and/or deacons?

Have I researched an answer to this question?
(For instance, is an answer to this question posted on a website or publication?)

Chapter Nineteen

What is the relationship between elders and/or deacons with the minister?

What is the relationship between the elders and/or deacons with the minister? This question functions as a continuation or follow-up to the previous question. First, what are the roles of elders and/or deacons? Second, what does the relationship look like between lay leadership and paid church staff? Every church must examine the roles and relationships. How do the roles and relationships need to be evaluated, or how are the roles and relationships structured in a healthy way? Some churches consider a paid senior minister as an elder, while others do not. Some consider paid staff as part of their eldership, while others do not.

With this question, the applicant is gaining a better understanding of the leadership of the church. Some applicants may not even want to ask this question, but I would gather as much information about the church as possible. If hired or the position is accepted on behalf of the applicant, then he or she will know a little more about the church, the roles, and relationships of leaders and volunteers. For an applicant who is looking to become the senior minister, this kind of a question may appear differently or bear different weight. To the applicant in some other capacity, he or she may not be as concerned. However, for the senior minister position, this needs to be clarified, so as to avoid any confusion or tension.

I ask this question to gain a better perspective on how decisions are made. Every church is unique and may be structured differently, so that is why I go ahead and ask this question. I have been on a church staff without inquiring about this, thinking that every church is the same. I learned very soon day to day operations were handled differently. Since then, I have investigated this and have come to see various roles and relationships each beneficial in their own respect.

Questions for reflection:
(Record your responses below.)

So tell me, what is the relationship between elders and/or deacons with the minister?

Why would I ask about this relationship?

Have I researched an answer to this question?
(For instance, is an answer to this question posted on a website or publication?)

Chapter Twenty

Is the minister expected to attend everything?

Is the minister expected to attend everything? This may seem like a strange question, but it does factor in what is expected of the minister. There are some churches that expect the minister to make an appearance or be at as many activities and functions as possible. Yes, the minister should be involved within the community; however, the church and its leadership should strive to support the minister to find a healthy boundary of time. The larger the church, the more possibilities of time demands, presence demands, time away from spouse and children, and absence from study and preparation.

An applicant should be seeking to determine whether healthy time boundaries are already in place or in need of establishing. This becomes extremely important if the applicant has a spouse and children. Too much time away from home can hinder ministry. Not enough time engaged in the community and making appearances can also hinder

Is the minister expected to attend everything?

ministry. This healthy time boundary also challenges the minister to develop other leaders and volunteers to step in and be available during the minister's absence.

I ask this question to determine a level of expectation. Does the church have a perspective of leadership development and delegation, or does the church rely solely upon the paid staff? I have found myself in a situation where the church expected me to be at as many public functions as possible, while maintaining strict office hours and organizing church activities. If I had a family during that time, then I would have not seen them that much. I desired delegation, but I felt the expectation was the opposite or even both. Healthy time boundaries became important for me to protect to keep my energy level and spiritual growth. There are seasons when more time is required, but an understanding should be in place to support rest and personal refreshment.

Questions for reflection:
(Record your responses below.)

So tell me, what are the minister's expectations?

Why would I ask about the minister's expectations?

Have I researched an answer to this question?
(For instance, is an answer to this question posted on a website or publication?)

Chapter Twenty One

Why did the last minister leave?

Why did the last minister leave? Some may look at this question and wonder who has the audacity to ask this? This question can shed light on the vacancy and current state of health of the church. If the predecessor left on bad terms, then there is likely tension and ill feelings. If the predecessor left on good terms, then there is likely positivity and hopefulness. There could be a combination of good terms with ill feelings and bad terms with hopefulness. There is also an unexpected departure that leaves a host of feelings behind. This is all the more reason to ask this question, to better gauge what the applicant may be walking into.

The applicant asks this question in either formal or informal settings. It may be asked by the applicant in a formal interview or amidst casual conversations in the interviewing process. An applicant seeks to observe and gather as much as possible, because one day the person in the same position will be exiting as well. The applicant may find himself or herself in a position short term or long term. When the departure comes, many of the same thoughts, feelings, and evaluations will be revisited and then the process will begin again.

I ask this question because the answer informs me and helps me to try and see what the people may be experiencing if I was in their shoes. If my predecessor retired, I may find sadness with the departure and excitement for the future, a bag of mixed feelings. This helps me see how to be and speak positive of the past along with the optimism of the future. While coming into an unstable environment, my presence may bring a sense of stability. In the church, we must be leading and guiding. We must reach out and build up. By understanding the past, a new future can be explored.

Questions for reflection:
(Record your responses below.)

So tell me, why did the last minister leave?

Why would I ask about the vacancy?

Have I researched an answer to this question?
(For instance, is an answer to this question posted on a website or publication?)

Chapter Twenty Two

Are there leadership development standards?

Are there leadership development standards? This is a combination of the requirements and qualifications for the vacant position to be filled as well as the expectations of the person in the position. Does the applicant meet the requirements and qualifications? Has the applicant received adequate education for the position and experience to fill the vacancy? Much of this is determined by the job posting and has already been reviewed. There are, however, instances where exceptions are made, so it should not discourage the applicant from applying. Besides, every applicant application and interview are new experiences because every church and applicant is unique.

An applicant should ask about leadership development standards to discern if the hiring church encourages its leaders to continue learning and growing even at the time of offering the position to an applicant. Skills are refined. New skills are learned. The church should be willing

Are there leadership development standards?

to support the leaders in this area. The leaders should support the volunteers too. Often at times, a learning organization is an enriching growing organization in many ways from quality to quantity and efficiency to effectiveness for professional staff and volunteers. The applicant should be continuing to find ways to develop as a leader and to be intentional about doing so. These may include mentors, coaches, reading books, listening to recordings, attending seminars and conferences.

I ask this question to determine if the church is willing to support my continual leadership growth and development. By supporting me in leadership development, the church is going to benefit as well. As new thoughts, ideas, and technologies emerge, it is an investment to learn about them and to integrate them within the position and, quite possibly, the church as well. This can become a win-win scenario.

Questions for reflection:
(Record your responses below.)

So tell me, does your church encourage leadership development?

Why would I ask about leadership development?

Have I researched an answer to this question?
(For instance, is an answer to this question posted on a website or publication?)

Chapter Twenty Three

How are polices developed?

How are policies developed? This question interacts with the by-laws and governance of the church. It is good to investigate the governing structure of the church. Does staff develop policies? Does lay leadership develop policies? Is it a combination of both? Is the senior minister responsible for creating the policies? Every church may handle this differently, so it would be wise to learn as much as possible. The larger size a church is, the more likely it is to have policies.

An applicant would need to become familiar with the policies, even as the applicant decides to accept the position or not. The church may not reveal certain policies until an applicant has officially begun. By asking questions, the applicant can become aware if policies exist and how those policies are developed. The applicant may not know specific written policies until the applicant is hired and officially begins in the role, which is risky and unfair. Depending upon the position, the applicant may or may not be involved in the policy making process.

I ask this question to see if there are any policies currently in existence. Once the answer has been established, then I move on to how policies are developed. This informs me of what tasks may need to be pursued in the future. Written documentation becomes helpful, so that all parties involved can be on the same page, being able to read and understand the policies. Policies can be revised at the appropriate time. Various factors affect the process. Policies, existent and non-existent, can be found. I have experienced a setting where policies were well documented, but hardly adhered to. This too affects the working environment. At times policies exist, but are not recorded. This can lead to frustration and tension because policies have not been communicated.

Questions for reflection:
(Record your responses below.)

So tell me, do you have formal policies?

Why would I ask about policies?

Have I researched an answer to this question?
(For instance, is an answer to this question posted on a website or publication?)

Chapter Twenty Four

How are policies implemented?

How are policies implemented? This question follows up to the previous question of how policies are developed. First, one must determine if policies exist. Second, one must determine how policies are developed. Thirdly, one must comprehend how those same polices are implemented. Who is ultimately responsible for establishing the policies and communicating them? The applicant gains a better understanding of how the vacant role assists with policy making.

The applicant needs to be aware of how the policies are implemented because he or she may be involved in the decision making process along with the communication process. One may see how this question relates to the expectations, job descriptions, and line of authority. It is validating to receive verbal confirmation and documentation of such things. When churches do not provide documented evidence, then verbal communication may be misconstrued. One thing may be stated, but practiced differently. This could be very frustrating for paid leaders. Upon

How are policies implemented?

personal reflection, one may conclude that if I had only asked this question, I would have responded differently.

I ask this question to discern consistency between having polices documented and implemented. I have seen policies well documented, but not implemented. When this happens, consistency does not exist, and it makes it difficult to build trust. For some, this may be focusing in on unnecessary details. For instance, if a small leak is not addressed, then the leak could cause bigger problems in the future. Policies can be helpful as long as they are implemented.

Questions for reflection:
(Record your responses below.)

So tell me, how are policies implemented?

Why would I ask about policy implementation?

Have I researched an answer to this question?
(For instance, is an answer to this question posted on a website or publication?)

APPENDIX

Checklist

Check box if question has been asked or discovered.	Question	Record response to question along with how and when the question was answered.
	What is the vision of the church?	
	What is the mission of the church?	
	What are the goals of the church?	
	What are the ministry teams?	
	What is the expected level of (member) involvement?	

Appendix

	What is the mission's (locally and/or globally) budget?	
	What are the three most important qualities of the church?	
	What does the church do well?	
	What is the church known for in the community?	
	How would you describe the health of the church?	
	How would you describe the demographic of the church?	
	What is the line of authority?	
	Is there a ministry budget to work from?	
	Is there a statement of faith?	
	Are there any major conflicts in the past?	
	What is the job description?	
	What is the organizational chart?	
	What is the role of elders and/or deacons?	

Checklist

	What is the relationship between elders and/or deacons with the minister?	
	Is the minister expected to attend everything?	
	Why did the last minister leave?	
	Are there leadership development standards?	
	How are policies developed?	
	How are policies implemented?	

www.ingramcontent.com/pod-product-compliance
Lightning Source LLC
Chambersburg PA
CBHW070326100426
42743CB00011B/2581